Meaningful Poems

Pan Poetica

Jørgen Panduro

Meaningful Poems

Pan Poetica

Books on Demand GmbH, Copenhagen,
Denmark

Cover: Idea, Jørgen Panduro - Graphics, Jimmy Machon
Publisher: Books on Demand GmbH, Copenhagen, Denmark
Print: Books on Demand GmbH, Norderstedt, Deutschland

ISBN: 9788743029496

The Author

Jørgen Panduro has a Master's Degree (MBC) Master's in Business Coaching with specialty in Protreptic, which is an old Greek art of conversation through concepts.

Jørgen, is the author of Pan Poetica (ISBN: 978-87-4302-709-6) which is a collection of poems mainly written in Danish. However, there are 11 poems written in English, 2 in German and 1 in Swedish.
It has the subtitle "Betydningens Digte" which is translated into "Meaningful Poems".

Jørgen, is co-author to the book, Things I Needed To Say, subtitle Poetic Conversations (ISBN 9788743029120).
Monica Lee is the other co-author. For more information about her please visit monicalee.me.

Prologue

"Meaningful Poems" is a poetry collection which touches on topics such as love, concepts, being, emotions, the soul, the spirit, beauty, life, behavior and the human being; topics that matter to most people to some degree.

The purpose of the poetry collection is to create reflection by putting words and meaning into the world we live and act in, with the phenomena that arises.

Furthermore, it is my hope that you can recognize or see yourself or your feelings in some of the poems. Perhaps, you may have an attitude towards it and maybe you will be inspired and motivated to write or put words into the thoughts you have.

There are opinions, attitudes, passions and emotions at stake. If they can be played up to their own minds and create reflection or just touch something in the soul, then the possibility that the elastic limits of perception can be shifted.

Creating value with reflection and meta-reflection can help create new panoramas, which have the potential to transcend the individual human being.

Content

A Sense of Freedom

The paradox of freedom is that it has boundaries – limitations
without the paradox you can´t define freedom – it is regulation
so, freedom exists only by virtue of its counterparts as
definitions

Freedom is conceived differently in which it is constructed
but, do we construct freedom or its counterpart in order to get
it conducted
seems like Jean Paul Sartre had it abducted

Freedom seems to be essential for human development and
transcendence
in freedoms shadows live - resistance to learn, lack of common
sense, bigotry, religion, ignorance, and dependence

We have to liberate freedom from its suppression
The good person will let peace, common sense, love, harmony
and humanity live in expression

You S`ay

A nation - so proud and sooo young
yet it considers itself so strong
a history with almost nothing but victory
but when you look closer is just a contradictory

In the name of freedom well-meaning and protective
it lacks the ability to be objective and reflective
suffering under religious stupidity, political greed, and
ignorance
the people are without liberty and it tends to be domestic
belligerence

So, the statue cries while holding high in oxymoronic suicide
This is a nation once leading the world – now bleeding
unable to see the wound, imbecility is killing the pride
The American Eagle has stretched wings and it is pleading

while the unfair political system has taken a hostage called
democracy
in the air, guns are sounding, and Stars and Stripes are waving
gently
watching claims of dignity through lies and hypocrisy
America, we still love you and we need you, but you must
change immensely

Undogmatic **S**ociety of **A**ffection

Longing

Thoughts and tears carried by longing
togetherness, humor and the third "I" in deprivation
emotional and soulfully falling
It´s hard to say goodbye in hugs and harmonic relation.

Pain and loss amplify affection
longing is a wild, deep feeling in search for connection
The empty spot is filled
the journey of longing is thrilled

Now I´m back again – with the dear
The heart finds beauty in sensuality
the spirit meta-reflects in liberty
That which seemed far away is now near

Grief

Is an immense proof of love and affection
Makes you see time in another dimension
Gives you wonderful moments of remembering with the
connection

Brings tears of missing to the ones you hold dear
Creates a melancholic state to be near those not here
Is when your heart sings the tune of reappear

Grief is clarifying behind your tears
The meaning does not cease through the years
To miss is to love, and real love never dies
The reflection it creates makes you wise

Your Hair

is expressive power
it puts your face in relief after taking a shower
enhances your grace in different and beautiful contours

is flirting and displays a seductive expression
gives an enticing feeling of obsession
brings different hairstyles that ensures

glances everywhere – you like them but just don´t care
shaking your head in a sexy way creates allurement – you are
aware
there you are, tempting, captivating creating emotions of
amours

Emptiness

A negative positive in infinity
Clean screen is something with nothing
Take a closer look – it is stunning

Emptiness operates memory in synergy

Inside emptiness exists creativity
On the outside anterior posterity
In between, doubt is fighting with reflection

Emptiness has inherent energy

You can never leave emptiness
It´s a circular regeneration
You need nothingness to avoid degeneration
Emptiness is a precursor for happiness

Emptiness is empty and contains nothing in everything

Age

Perception of age should be a beautiful thought
confirmed by birthdays it´s a timeframe we are taught

Age is existence and possess meaning
operates as a natural displacement while you´re breathing
linearity is only a perception

Embrace life as an extension
how you exist should be your intention

Age
is the wear and tear of life and being
Age
is a patinated artwork of dreaming

Live Now

A sweet melancholy fills your heart
flashbacks and memories create the art
of your life as a vivid perspective
it´s significant to be reflective

You live your life - or?
Do it now – make a roar
No unconscious course
Life is beautiful – find the source

Genuine - essential to be
in the meeting with me
it´s value to your identity
it shows in your entity

The Expected Anticipation

When you anticipate it´s not too late
it´s the joy, happiness and bliss that leads
in naive excitement for your needs
to be disappointed is a risk and a fate

It´s the connotative difference you need to see
expectation is a catalyst for reflection
the anticipation is what you want the future to be
either way it is a projection

anticipation is the concept, it is the concept you feel
denotation is the truth it´s got meaning
connotation is the array, it´s the expectation, the deal
preconception is how we are perceiving

Misty Tirades of Gratitude

It is becoming more and more rare
seems like people just don´t care
The impact it has on the heart
it´s being taken for granted and drifting apart

Gratitude -
if you knew the value, you would know the

magnitude -
that is the force of the word it possesses and the

attitude -
is how authentic and sincere you show the

solicitude –
which lies in the concept of gratitude

Solitary

I´m alone in your soul when I speak
being ignored is like taking a hit on the cheek

    I feel frustrated and powerless – I am unhappy and blue

I´m abandoned when you are condescending to me
shouting and emotional abuse wants me to flee

    The spark in my soul is about to leave my view

My spirit, misses freedom even if it is deserted
I have to find the passage back to myself – be diverted

    I have had enough, it´s my life – I want to live

Leaving egocentrism, bigotry, and misery
I want to be the writer of my history

    I´m coming home

Fame Fatale

People's awareness of something fantastic
achievement by hard work painted in authentic colors
to balance the reputation can be overly dramatic

Idolization has a price – you´re in focus and have to behave
in search for recognition - or humble and hide
either way, you´re the people's slave

Fame obliges but you decide
in the spotlight where you are framed
how to live with the pride

Mama

Grieving so much
if just I could have one more touch
You were already cold, but looked so at peace
it was devastating to watch your breathing cease

Standing there looking at your grave which is unknown
but with all the flowers you finally got a throne
It's hard to say goodbye without tears in my eyes
my mind goes back in time – remembering all the good things
– while my soul cries

Mama, I just miss you so
I wish I spent more time, but now I have go
Mama, your light just died
your smiling face I will recall with pride

Rose Grip

means everything it´s soreness with cream
when the blood flows from your hand down your wrist

Penetration in the skin – the thorns – the dream
the pain is anesthetized by affection to be kissed

The flower, the leaves of red
so beautiful they epitomize the things I said

When the rose is handed to your lover
you will feel the pain until you discover
the color red on her cheek resembles the rose
the soul resonates – it´s the right one you chose

Transcending Bike Rides

Firm grip at the brake handles, leaning in forward position
enjoying the sound of the smooth and reliable mechanics
I enjoy the sun, the air in my hair – I make a transition

Remembering Kraftwerk's Tour de France
the melody and the inciting rhythm set me in a trance

My heart is pulsating my breath is elevated
the sun gives me the light sighted view – it is captivated

The sum of the bike mechanics and the physical environment
the power, watt, muscle action put in to my own requirement
It gives me -

> The feeling of freedom mode
> Takes me down a nostalgic road
> Power through melancholy
> Sound pleasure from the machinery
> A state of overcoming
> It is simply stunning

Overall, it transcends my soul to an ecstatic place where
everything is clear

Driving a Painting

I´m driving through the metropolis
restless – can´t focus on the road of my life
seems clear but not in sight
I´m not scared but lost in Heliopolis

with different speeds and directions
I try to find peace and the one
everything is so bright in the sun
but I tend to misinterpret the intersections

The picture comes forward as a mystery
it´s hard to objectify the canvas from this position
I have to go meta and reconsider my mission
I want to show the painting as my history

I drive through the city of lights with my brushes
my direction paints my life – my existence
my mind is clear, my soul is near, I see the distance
I feel peace, I see the one I want to give crushes

Cry Cry American Regime

Your people show and hide their tears
it´s your creation of fictive fears

> symbolized in riots, religious madness, driven by
> power and greed

Mr. Politician you should be ashamed
with hidden agendas and neglect that is proudly proclaimed

> all of it followed by a strained smile when you
> illegally intercede

Mr. Congressman are you worthy, are you authentic?
personal influence surpasses people's interest – are you
dysgenic?

> political games, compromised strategy, and tactics –
> is that how you lead?

The political system pretends to listen to the people's voice
in reality, they are given no choice

> they are too blind to see that America bleeds

Bye bye American lie

The Journey in the Swing

You and I swinging together while happiness sings
in our heads we hear the same song
the melody takes us along
the mesmerizing path, and the future rings

The journey in the swing brings us near
the place where shadows invite to the light
we swing in harmony, the same pace, the height
we have big smiles – there are no worries no fear

The feeling is breathtaking into the picture
that were once taken and now we sit here
with the same smile – I´m the cavalier
you are the lady - and this is our scripture

The Invitation

I invite you to –

a conversation that is meaningful and dilates
a dialogue with depth and weight
be yourself with naked mind and unfold

                                        hold

I invite you to -

dare challenge yourself, with reflective thoughts - an idea
to let me be your hostage so you can practice sophia
find an empty space for your "I"

                                        my

I invite you to -

transcend your thoughts with me untied
see the beauty of the intersubjective ride
reach for the synthetic and fragile creation land

                                        hand

I invite you to -
come home and see the difference
to hold our hearts for a moment to sense reverence
relax after your mind has been extended

                                        intended

I invite you to -

bend your thoughts – to what is beyond the extreme
go inside and discover the most immanent dream
be curious – to search for happiness and freedom

I invite you to -

The Offended Violation

To think you have the right to be offended
is a justification of egocentrism and stupidity
it is the lack of the ability to see reality as it is intended
it is a behavior where you disregard responsibility

It makes no sense, and where is your dignity
grow up, be authentic – don´t drown real violation
don´t be the example of bigotry
think about what is being said, and do the translation

It´s not all about you

His Eyes

Inside myself - all over the world - even in space
suddenly out of nowhere and everywhere I saw this face
captivated, breathtaking - it was all in his eyes
I haven´t even touched him, yet I lay at night and my heart
cries

Eyes of blue, cold water, fresh air, clear as sincerity
radiation of calmness, stoic like he is taking me in
there is no resistance – I see everything in clarity
his spirit has taken my heart – I feel my skin as a sin

Pierced by his gaze I give in - I let him in
I´m being seduced but he is not aware
a cosmic love story is about to begin
he is in love with me, but he doesn´t know it yet – he is having
an affair

yet, unconsciously but still so vivid – I´m still seduced by his
eyes

Last Night

Last night
I talked to love – to get wiser – to be able to know

Last night
I walked with love – I wanted to spend time
I wanted to understand to hear the chime

Last night
I listened to the notes of love – to hear it echo
while listening to Wagner's Tristan and Isolde – it sounded
mellow
the sound of love seduced me in allegretto

Last night
I painted love – it was sitting on a note in front me
it was blurry but it wanted me to see
it caressed my fragile soul with tenderness
and whispered you will find me some day – I´m not endless

The Book

I sensed a book – that´s something
it´s about everything
so also about nothing

The book is a panoramic sensation
I see everything in the desolation
I read it in the house of contemplation

It has no author – no pages – no sense
it consumed me; it was so tense
I realized it had no commence

Wires and Connection

Different colors of wires
coming out of your head
the beauty is alienating like dread
locks you to the future code of desires

you are connected to the universe
you can hear the composition of sounds
it forms a melody and lyrics with no bounds
like a firecracker in transverse

you have tapped into an orchestra
yellow magic is synesthesia – you see the music
the rhythms fills your body it´s so lucid
you have embraced my neologism "musicoetry" to registrar

In the Shadow of Your Shade

Don´t hide in your shadow
it´s a self-deception you show
you are hiding yourself in transparency
what you don´t see is the errancy

The phantom of the self-esteem
guides you to your dream
to hide in the clear dark is a figment
it´s a spiral of descent

You will become a wraith, an eidolon
find your true spirt and decide upon
to walk out of your shadow remaining you and your "I"
when you are truly yourself, you will fly

Screen Love

Love in the 21st century
vibes and feelings through cyberspace
it´s hard to maintain serenity

Longing so desperately – trying not to show
love can be so intense through deep conversations
one day we will meet at the end of the rainbow

   - then love will explode and continue to expand in other
dimensions – just like the universe
   - grand love will have its own existence - transcending
energy – in which we will immerse

I will love you till the end of time
and when I´m no longer around, you can read the rhyme –

Meta "I"

There you walk - looking down at your "I"
you have an intention and its extensional
you miss the importance of being intensional
have you ever asked yourself why?

In relationships you observe your "self"
it can be surprising and may not be consistent
with what you thought about your "self" in existence
but you see - it is in itself

Metaphorically speaking - it is your eye
Metamorphose your "self" and "I"
    - try to be metaethical

When You Are Talking with Your Eyes

The emptiness, the depth, the vastness, the colour
your eyes drag me in, they whisper to my mind
The dark pupils dancing invitation makes me stutter
They see my soul – even the sides that are blind

I need to hear what they say - do they want me to stay
They pulsate and glow, but how will I know
I can´t stop looking at, and into your eyes wherever we lay
they shine like a painting from Michelangelo

Please darling, talk to me with your eyes
They speak the language of truth and they hypnotize

Music for the Advances

It is the sense of the whole sound picture
to hear and feel the individual instruments
the overwhelming of the interplay - the mixture
the lyrics composition and intents

    - it´s like it soothes my soul
    - the music says – let me show you the world with my eyes

The synthetic resonances are chiming in the air
beats transcend into energetic movements
nodes dancing with lyrics, that make you aware
and the refrain sounds again and again – need no
improvements

    - listening to the mesmerizing melodies – gives me new life
    - the rhapsody that embraces and covers me in symphony

When Eudaimonia Holds Hands with Sophia and Phronesis

Is when

You are feeling happy and overjoyed
evilness is repressed and destroyed

you love your life and live it to the full extent
your soul gives a special scent

openness of your heart is immense
you love unconditionally and intense

you are able to rest in yourself and show serenity
being aware of your entity

spirit and soul sitting together in emptiness and radiates
creating your identity in which your "I" resonates

your authentication transcends into a third "I" with new
dimensions
you will be able see and hear your thoughts through the
other's extensions

Café Honesty

At Café Honesty I can´t buy

    here I must make myself deserving
    it is my essence to be incurving
    if I want to catch the giving from the honesty of merging

At Café Honesty I sit alone

    in company with my entity
    here I seek of honest identity
    listening to the resonance in its brutality

At Café Honesty I wonder

    between honesty and dishonesty what is the glow
    is it a clearing where I find love to show
    with meaningful love I have everywhere to go

At Café Honesty I don´t sit anymore

    I have gone with honesty and I smiled
    back to the place where I was a child
    there I will meet freedom and be reconciled

Pan-scription

It is implicit in the word
rhetoric, poetry, transcending conversations
infinity in dialogues perpetuated in associations

Descriptions, analysis, assessments are transferred
poetry's play with words and concepts
superior through the unconventional, it allows prospects

Expressions that give imprints are referred
the essential is triumphant and clarifying
the meaningful is glorifying

The Missing Dialectic

Looking at the world it seems so polemical
constructive dialogues are replaced by harsh discussions
it´s like a missing theater stage for common ground in a
musical
and the religious, political, and cultural fights have serious
negative repercussions

The lost art of dialectic seems to be replaced by manipulative
diplomacy
the stupidity holds hands with greed and power, disguised as
action and suspicious results
they claim it as victory
but the only effect is repulse

Dialectic manners are a necessary quality, and one must want
the dialectic
instead of egocentric behavior, it should be a search for
common meaning
the world is going into singularity with devastating
consequences – it´s opposite eclectic
mankind can be disappointing, but it´s not too late even
though we are bleeding

Transatlantic

Love transatlantic
non-physical even though so romantic
From storms to mermaids
antenna, satellite and amazing web dates

Pulsating messages in joy and a tear
spirits playing have nothing to fear
The longing fuels the ecstatic
when they melt it will be gigantic

To Become

How do you become?
When you become – you happen, when you happen you
change
to become happens – it´s a question of consciousness and
range

You become in consciousness, relationship, language and
conversations
When you are being said, the saying should have your genuine
attention
when the saying is being said, it opens up for the possibility of
extension

The consciousness of our own being is a catalyst for becoming
You can lift the said to a higher context and be the saying in
the conversation
with attention on the conversation within the conversation –
you will become - revelation

The Transparent Mirror

You are looking at the mirror´s transparency
you are getting lost in its apparency
it reflects your soul, and your spirit is whispering gently
do you dare to see your "I" – it must be intensely

What do you see in the transparent reflection
if you look closer you will change your perception
When the mirror engulfs you with its brightness
you will discover your true "I" in your selfness

Take Me

Don´t take me as I am, but as what I could be
Take me in - inhale me, I´ll be your friend if your soul can see
Take a chance on me and I will make you free

If you take me – be sure that you are ready for a rush
Taken are the souls that resonate when they have a crush
when you take me I will give in and blush

If you can catch me and make love to my existence
I will catch your fall in my arms with no resistance
catching love can be done even from great distance

Take me
Take me

Take me to your "I" so I can find myself

The Eternal Life Errands

Did you run an errand for your mother?
Were you proud and is it something for each other?
An errand is that something for which you would bother?

In an errand lives meaning and sense – you just have to feel
might do it with pride and with honest intentions to help – it´s
real
by doing errands you become yourself through the other, it´s
non-ego ideal

When you stop doing errands, you slowly fade away
your becoming through the others, takes away some of your
existence - you get gray
stay vibrant and energetic and keep doing errands till your last
day

I still do errands for mother even though she passed away
several years ago -

The Flexible Thought

Bending your thoughts is reflection
it´s a constant smoldering curiosity
it´s seeing the world in panorama and reciprocity
it´s lateral thinking with direction

Pre-reflection is -
    challenge of consciousness
    healthy food for your mind
    positive energy with openness
    never behind

When did you last hear a flexible thought?
What is the substance of a flexible thought?
If a flexible thought is empty – what does it contain?
Which vibrations do you feel when having a flexible thought?
Who is the nearest relative to a flexible thought?
What is on the outside of a flexible thought?

Is This a Meme?

Creating a meme
ensures the possibility of existence through time
the phenomenon constructed could be a rhyme
depending on human actions and behavior to stream

Memes are innovative imitations
distorted to perfection
Memes are manipulatively aimed
it´s only purpose is survival to be famed

Remember to be critical because it seems
that often there is a hidden agenda in memes
where genes are biological memes are cultural
a positive outcome depends on the moral

Dance the Disease

One step aside and kick
the disease – you have to be quick
step, step touch embrace the disease
it´s easier to control and make it cease

Tango the sickness - you decide
even though it affects you – you dance with pride
the symptoms that shows, you waltz with ease till it slows
the malady is only a melody which you need to swing on your
toes

dancing – positive movements and mental extension
that may help you keep the condition in detention
but sometimes it practices coercing
but at least you were dancing

Choose Your Life

Find the infinity in the finality
freedom will appear as a desirable ghost
you must be driven by fervor and host
severity, effort, and emotionality

Is this way of life aesthetic or ethic?
All dressed up and everywhere to go
only the wise will reflect the thought to flow
if you lead your pen with sincerity you might be poetical

When you have chosen your life, chose how to live
focus your "I" to others and give
you are alive – to live is a paradox
if you want to transcend – be heterodox

The Mirror of Life

When looking in the mirror of life – what do you see?
When life mirrors you and you mirror life – what will you be?
How deep do you dare to look, to see your true reflection in
the mirror
if you are authentic and honest you will get your "self" nearer

The reflected personality is only half the reality
are you able to see your soul or is that too much emotionality
life is measuring you constantly – the premise is a condition
you shouldn´t miss it – it could be your admission

to see your "self" live in life, in the reflected image
when you sharpen your consciousness, you will realize it´s a
privilege

Tango the Dialectic

Verbal dancing led by searching minds
moving forward shift in steps create concepts of all kinds
the consciousness is contemplating – what will it find

to be reflected further – thesis, antithesis functions as a
catalysis
the concept becomes extended, bended and forms a synthesis
the words, expression and conversation almost constitute a
verbal kinesthesis

By now the dialectic dances even more beautifully and with
wonderful grace
the dialogue and the event gets its own life and space
when the dance is over – everything falls into place

Lots of Vibrant Ecstasy

It has a vast depth and light
The meaningfulness is so right
The feelings it gives makes you profoundly bright

It can make you ecstatic, madly devoted, occurs at the in- and outside of your feelings – it has a certain vibration that resonates with the being.

You want it so much
It makes you want to touch
When you feel it, it gives you a rush

When it happens you get blind but see clearer, your judgment gets weaker, but your awareness sharpens, and your devotion radiates with immense energy.

You feel proud and humble for this event -
grateful, giving and extended for ascent
if you were asked – you would give assent

In its essence it is life-giving and soul filling. You can let your spirit free as a shield that radiates positivity and affection like an injection of rapture.

You are there – it lives in you – it´s immanent
you have access to humanity and see its power – it is eminent
It´s just so incredibly magnificent

The Delicate Flower

As a heliotropic creature she moves to the light
showing all the beautiful colors she possess
they can change in the shade as she dresses
with the right amount of water, she will increase in emotional
height

She enjoys the rain falling on her fragile leaves
like pearls falling down to her feet
the shower from the sky is what she needs
and she allows some of it in her cleaves

The attractive flowerhead is protected by thorns
her body is curvy and flexible – it gives her shape
among all the other flowers – she is standing out in the
landscape
treat her right, and she will wait – even in storms

The flower is called Nica Pulchritudo

While You Slept

You were
in my thoughts and mind
smiling so gracefully and kind
giving me that look that only in you I can find

I imagined
to see you in reality
to hold you, caress you, smell your sexuality
a life with you in emotionality

we
danced together in the night
we made love under the dimmed light
contemplating in poems that we recite

Both of us
gave each other that look – and we knew
that our life would have a panoramic view
and we whispered – I love you

Tell Me Your Story

I promise to listen with curiosity
I will be your sanctuary
I will let you feel security

Tell me more – and create your "self"

Your life fascinates me, even though it is nothing unique
it is the way you speak, your feelings, energy, and empathy
you tell with such an intensity that I want to seek

Tell me more – I can see the picture

The conversation, the narrative, gets its own life in perspective
the soul is on flow and orchestrates the dramaturgy
Me being reflective and you subjective

Please tell me more – I am seduced with your charm and
radiation – you have my admiration

I Found

Myself in the city of distress
as a grown up, I was still a child
my intention with life crashed and had no one to caress
wrong choices and I was exiled

The love was still there and for my child everywhere
time went on with the same style
when I realized I had something to share
I had been running down the wrong aisle

I had to move my mind, told by my soul
it had always been there, and most people loved, it I think
but I never was a whole
now my soul and mind are in sync

Regrets there have been a lot in the city of pop
in the atmosphere where I thought I was on top
Edith Piaf sings - Non, je ne regrette rien
I am trying to be a better man

This Book

Is
intentional
invitational
maybe sensational
conditional of perception, reflection and abstract ability

educational
unconventional
through meaning relational
emotional at times if you use empathy and sympathy as a
capability

tensional
fusional
behind the lines and words connotational
some rhymes are aphoristic, some arouse wonder and some are
confrontational

The Empty Room of Feelings

In the room it is dark because light is
you feel light – all senses are open in the proprioceptive mode
you perceive the surroundings that perceive you are
in the room, the revelation reveals the empty spot where you
are nothing in yourself

The room is a semi-ghost and your host
you are the room when it is empty with most
you look back at the door, but don´t know how you got in
the colors couldn´t be better arranged in the dark spin

You just entered, but been there for years
the perception of your memory brings you to tears

emergence is reality and the room provides you with sensuality
you are seduced by nothing, your spirit is free – it is
renewability

You Found What You Were Looking for

It´s incredible what you did
I didn´t even know that we fit

Your charm and eyes had an impact
the abstract and vivid mind made contact

The search for love and affection – just being understood
I felt you like a hungry and neglected soul lost in the wood

"Crimson Tears" was the first sign – you felt connected
finally, someone from far away heard your voice – you were
detected

A lifetime of waiting for the love you had yearning
a spark, words that were spoken, and your heart was
confirming

that what we now share is special in many ways
the search is over, I´m yours you don´t have to chase
just be yourself, and let me look at your lovely face
we collided in space, and now our hearts are at place

Face of Tears

There you stand looking up crying with a begging face of tears
trying to talk at the same time, but it is too burdensome
you are hurt and need consolation, someone to take away your
fears

I sense the hurting as a feeling of injustice and despair
you need to be hugged, kissed and feel that someone cares
it seems your loving heart doesn´t understand that some
people can be unfair

Come here my love, you can trust me - I´m your shield
just let it all out, slowly stop crying and let me hold you
we will solve this together, let me caress your heart – just smile
and you will be healed

In-spiration

Breathe in the spirit colorless like the air
Exhale the CO_2 the essence has stayed in there
Respirate in thoughtfulness and contemplating everywhere

Inspiration is inhaled from the outside and formed on the inside
processed, transformed and created it can be applied
something happens when ideas collide

Inhale the emptiness as room for reflection
find the spirit in the essence of imperfection
In-spiration you will find the affection

Move and Forward

Standing still does not exist – you know
life is in a constant flow
it accelerates like a turbo

Having a break, time out or a holiday
life still moves and you can´t hide away
even a mental retreat is an election Thursday

yes – mental and spiritual disembarkation
is needed, it is a donation
to yourself and the effect is transcending

Yet, it is still a move forward, a parallel stimulation
making you agile, stronger, wiser in aspiration
that you can keep up the move in acceleration

Temptation

Is a precondition for existing and not insisting
is the a catalyst for inspiration and yearning
for life – you just have to feel it – it should be persisting

To be tempted is normally used in a superficial way
have you ever thought of being tempted by life?
Think about it in its essence – put it on display

?
If you are not tempted by life – do you live?

If existence itself isn´t in focus, how can you feel yourself?

Is taking life for granted in reality a denial of life?

Is your life a miscomprehension, or is it fulfilled,?

Do you strive for life to have quality in a meta perspective?

- be tempted

She Moved

you didn´t - you kept your negativity
for her it felt like captivity

She tried to make you listen – to be heard
but all you could hear was your own word

She showed you love and devotion
in return you gave her ignorance when she needed emotion

She did not leave you – you left her long ago
it was her only choice to show
that you were too egocentric and selfish
in her view you will slowly diminish

She moved on to a happier life in love perspective
for the one that shows her true love, she will not be rejective

Crimson Tears

running slowly down my cheek
it´s the love from you I seek
where are you – you hold my soul
I´m trembling, I shiver – you have control

My heart is pulsating, and my crimson tear
color my spirit - when will you be near
close against my body – a gentle touch
wherever you are, I need you so much

In despair I search my soul and the light
thinking of you and hold us so tight
our naked bodies in ecstatic exploration
they magnetize, they sparkle with no hesitation

Where are you my darling? I want you in me
Without your energy I can´t be

My crimson tear holds you dear –

Love in the Moment's Creature

is a telling and intense look
when you have the feeling that you´re on the hook
you wanted to give your heart – which he took

is when time stands still in a kiss
when his presence is not near and you miss
the point where your life feels like a bliss

intense love makes climax a shivering explosion
when a touch feels like soothing lotion
it becomes natural to show devotion

holding hands means something
a look at your love makes your heart start pumping
a hug feels touching

Find your love creature

A Ticket to Be

is a ticket you cannot buy
it is all about your I

Through decent behavior it can be approved
to keep its value – it must continuously be improved

Take good care of your ticket - it will be
your identification for everyone to see

One day your ticket will be your legacy
a standard for compliance - it will live endlessly

Supermodel

She stands with an empty look - the consciousness is seduced
the body shines, the brain confines – she´s an excuse

Beauty is a product that is easy to sell
the hungry horny looks, is a repulsive smell

She gets styled, dresses up, and hides behind her shield
where is she going – she knows she is a yield
The girl behind the facade isn't intriguing
doesn't anybody see her? She is also a human being

Greedy capitalism creates haute couture on heels high
The cover girls rocking their hips, flash a thigh
As a consumer product she belongs to the crowd´s eye

The fragile figure overturns on stage, blood is running from
her nose
The fragility is exposed to the horny looks – they will gladly
pay for another pose

Robot, slave, whore
the model is still lying on the floor

The Life of Death

Death – were you stillborn when you already were dead – I
mean can you die as dead?
Death you live when you die, therefore you have life – it´s
dread.

Death hasn´t any dignity – death is reactive
Not living, in the dark light is attractive

The prefix" death" is amplifying – highlighting as a negative
- oxymoron as a positive

Life exists
Death insists

Death you are not comfortable to write about – you seem so
distant
but we will meet some day, when my soul no more is resistant

Freedom Dances with Beauty

Freedom gives beauty life and ember
beauty is never dead - but it can be suppressed
it depends on the concept in which it´s dressed
there is beauty in the unbeauty as well – remember

When beauty dances it is contagious
freedom is beautiful it takes away fear
it is so breathtaking that it´s outrageous

They dance to the sound of satisfaction
and the melody of attraction

The music is transcending and -

The Poisoning Isms

Fundamentalism

Racism

Islamism

Radicalism

Creationism

Narcissism

Fanatism

Fascism

Chauvinism

Theism

is dragging the world downwards in a malicious, vicious, and imbecile path – stick to the positive isms.

A Telephone Call with Love

Hello – is this love?

Yes, this is love!

Hi love - Is it hard to exist in the world today?

Well I do exist in everyone, but in great parts of the world, I have been shot down by indoctrinated ignorance in a malicious and morbid way.

When do you thrive?

I thrive when peace, love, harmony and mutual respect is present – also called humanity – then I am alive.

Who are your companions?

I have a lot of companions, but the ones that reinforce me most are freedom, justice, truth, and beauty – they are my bastions

Love is -

Yes love is

Tabula Rasa

is necessary through your entity
in order not to lose your identity

To clean the board can be liberating
almost exhilarating
It induces a clearer view - new energy
you will be able to see the meaning in entropy

Erase connections with bad energy and hate
find the substance and get your shit straight

The act of tabula rasa will show you revelation
and life as a wonderful temptation

Move forward and erase
and you will find yourself in grace

White Sheet

Sitting in front of a white sheet
and yet indifference comes down on the paper
thrown on like a dress with excess draper
my brain is stuck in Poetry Street

Is indifference worse than nothing?
Is this poem without content?
Maybe it´s subconscious intent
It could be it´s pure stuffing

Suppose I´m at an empty place
from where I can embrace
the contemplating state
that will make me concentrate
on poetry as transcending thoughts in rhymes
one that makes you wonder through times
a reflection on the process
that might lead to progress

Social Dys-media

Often without great consideration
attitudes and opinions are aired
sometimes it´s hard to see the causation

MeToo has gotten a carte blanche
it has gotten out of hand and has impaired
the constructive conversation in advance

The keys are glowing in anger, apathy and personal attacks
the result is unreflected opinions shared
please – just think before you write, before you get caught in
your syntax

Write your post with consideration and reflection
be varied and invite to critical open conversation
it is okay to get your opinions oxygenated
just be sure that you were thinking before you advocated

The Newborn Neologism

Once it will appear
when the right concepts are near
foreplay will be redundant – needless
their attraction will sparkle – just speechless

it's the magnetic raw, no doubt feeling
deep look in the eye non-concealing
moment in which the concepts know
the next step will be a kiss of glow

So intense, so immersive that the soul will excite
love and devotion to make love – passionately
until they explode in a new height
and they fall into each other romantically

From the lovemaking collision of the two concepts a
neologism is born -
transaffectionarity

Attention Whore

Contempt for other people in the hunt for fame
ego driven femme fatale that has no shame

Strategic manipulation with employees is Number One
the company will suffer when she is done

With envy in her hand, bigotry becomes a precondition
low self-esteem is a catalyst for her inhibition

Using power to manifest herself and her name
in the act if she fails, the other ones will get the blame

Attention whore – Pussy Galore
Revealed and displayed – no one will adore

The Four Driving Forces

A precondition for the good Conversation is -

Orexis - Greek for appetite – you have to possess a certain curiosity, appetite and attention

Ousia - Greek for substance or essence – it´s about the essential, the true being to reach another dimension

Theoria – Greek for behold and in Latin it´s contemplation – the ability to stay in a thinking state - reflection

Thaumazain – Greek for wonder – it´s being imaginative, to see and feel the wonder - a mind extension

The Soul of the Floor

Floor you are worn
Floor you have been here since I was born
Your patina shows the wear and tear of life
Floor you are always near
Floor you don't complain when I spill my beer

Platform for stature
Basis for home
My shadow as contour
You carry me when I write a poem

Floor - now I am no more – please take care
Floor - so beautiful you shine – it´s you I wear
Now I am lying on you lifeless with a stiff glance
Floor - thanks for the last dance

Apparency Dinner

There I am at the restaurant ordering
dinner for me and for my date wondering
why she isn´t there when I can see her face
just in front of me at her place

The waiter brings my beer
I take a sip, and she is still here
I love the way she looks in the shimmering light
the dinner has arrived and I´m hungry for life

There is no one to talk to at restaurant temptation
even though I have a conversation
apparency is the format, the imagination
I finished my dinner, but there is no flirtation

The Paralyzed Life

Solidified opinions

create trivial and apathetic conditions

No variations only repeat

Everyday logic is dominating

the continuous and automated repetition only makes it

aggravating

you put your existence to sleep

No urge for wisdom no curiosity

if you don´t grab life, you show no generosity

You have to constantly see yourself as incomplete

Don´t pretend, you have to transcend

your existence has to extend   .

it is yourself you have to meet

An Invitation to Observe Your Life

What does responsibility want?
Is honesty something you will haunt?

How do you see the importance of sincerity?
In your existence – is there generosity?

If you get a visit from love – how much will you open?
Is empathy a concept you have chosen?

Do you pursue understanding?
Do you feel your wisdom is expanding?

How do you value the concept of altruism?
Do you consider humanity as synergism?

Is emptiness a place where you practice contemplation?
When life ceases to exist – can that be a celebration?

Would Your Conscience Fall in Love?

Conscience – is what you know with yourself – a store of your
life
it contains things you show and things you hide
some is with pride and some where you cried
what will die with you in your afterlife

To fall in love takes an open mind
you have to show true affection
if you want a limitless connection
to hide too much is leaving love behind

If your conscience is able to fall in love
you have to forgive yourself for what must be weighing you
down
if you want to be dressed in love´s gown
your conscience will extend above

yourself

Electronic Consciousness

Like a soundwave so soft
listening in the dark you get lost
in beautiful tones and sounds
you feel your soul surrounds

the things that matter – that is significant
when the diamond rolls in the vinyl – it´s a stimulant

Game on - the peaks of the rhythm flows
Soft Wave will compose
The yellow vinyl spins and spins in steady state
it takes you to a place to contemplate

There is a synthetic reality it´s Soft Wave
the more you listen the more you crave

Be with Me

and contemplate
together we will create
thoughts and reflections

and get curious on existence
we will both walk the distance
our catalyst is imperfections

and be in awe of the emptiness
you and I will transcend our consciousness
it´s a place to grow and evaluate perceptions

and in humanity embrace
ideas and conceptions with grace
which in substance and essence is affections

The Beautiful Arches

Concentric arches with
same emptiness point in infinity
- we are all going there, but is it with dignity?

You feel small when you walk to the point – but
as you get older the arches seem reduced
In life – we are all seduced

In search for peace the distance feels heavy and
to obtain freedom you have to fight the evil power
The beautiful arches give peace and quiet a hand
you can do that, if you meet the other with a flower

When you get near the infinite point of emptiness
make sure when you look back it was with kindness

Misused Helpfulness

With a smile she gives everything
her heart grows calm when she sees the smiles
to give, she will tirelessly walk the miles
She will be there when life gives you a sting

Her soul thrives when she helps and gives
for the ungrateful, she will forget herself to live

When she doesn´t receive anything back
she hides her heart and forgets it also has needs
while her light slowly burns out - she proceeds
her soul is at risk for a heart attack

Over time she will vanish, she won´t even be missed
in return all she ever wanted was her soul to be kissed

Painting the Future

In your living room there is a painting
it´s a painting that is constantly changing

Suddenly you realize, you´re the one creating the ritual
you literally generate the eventual
the brush is your mind, your imagination
do not seek for any explanation

You can´t see it, but it is conceivable
you are behind in the front – supposable

You need to look for the emergence
The past and the present was the future, but now divergent
While you paint you must grab the appearance
with your mind in two dimensions, you´ll see the coherence

You paint yourself into destiny
mind stretching the Deja-vu into transcendency

In your living room there is a painting
it´s a painting that is constantly changing

The House of Infinity

The door is open in a closed monument
it´s easy to get in but it takes encouragement

Once in, you can feel what you see
It´s incomprehensible, but a place you want to be

Silence is sounding in the air and gives you tranquility
you are breathless and feel admirability

Your heart gets a rest and your mind unwinds
the spirit takes your hand it´s unconfined
you left a valuable monument behind
now you´re praised for being kind

Read

so humanity will survive
knowledge and wisdom will thrive

with open criticism and perceptions
find the significant in imperfections

different subjects and broaden your mind
for those who are mentally blind

with your heart and devotion
to keep your spirit in motion

love into a daily cohesion
compassion into composition

Read

The Truth in the Lie

The truth is expected
a lie is not respected
The hypocrisy is, that a lie is accepted
when the truth is neglected

Innocent truth and white lies
hold hands with the purpose of protection
some might say gentle selection
 in the end, it´s the narrator that determines the prize

The truth in the lie is a convenient manipulation
it´s a social and cultural coherence
it works as a conform euphemism, in cultivation
almost like a meme disguised as a beauty in appearance

Seen from Above

It´s almost like a natural disaster
Humanity acts like it is the master

Looking down we created so many beautiful things
still our behavior – it´s not difficult to be ashamed
both for loving deeds and evil intentions we can be blamed
the nature will show us, that we are not the kings

Humanity still has the chance, but it demands:

That we unite and put aside rigid dogmas and beliefs
it is all about how we perceive
the world that is given us to habitate
why can´t we just collaborate -

Are evil intentions humanity?
Are we acting in sanity?